Contents

Some words are shown in bold, **like this**. You can find out what they mean by looking in the glossary.

River of mystery

The River Nile is the longest river in the world at 6,650 kilometres long. It travels through ten African countries. It is made up of two main rivers – the White Nile and the Blue Nile.

The Nile Delta is where the River Nile spreads out and goes into the sea.

Nile Delta

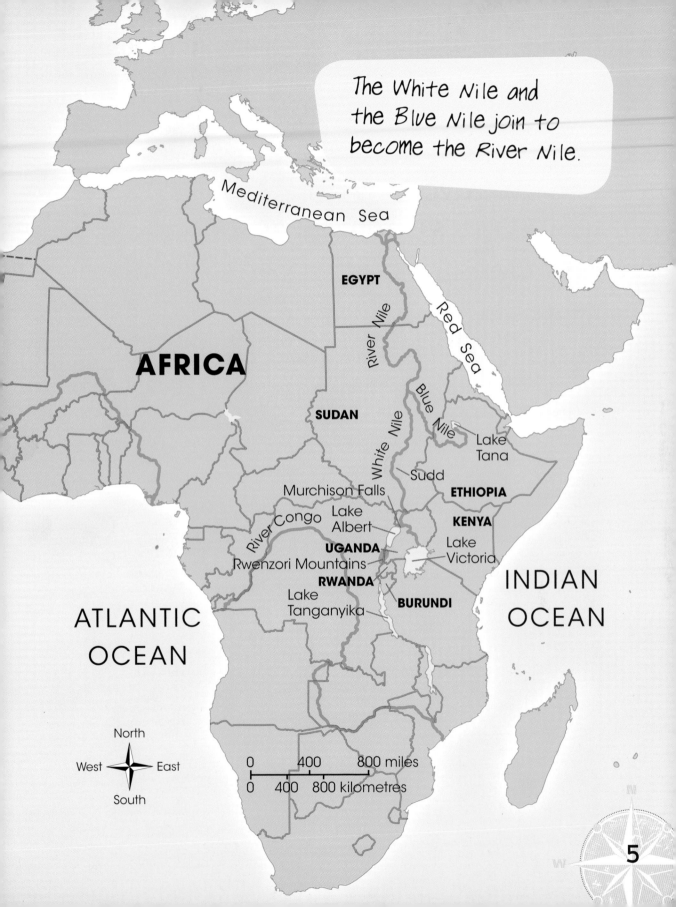

The River Nile floods every year. The floods make the land nearby very good for growing **crops**. The ancient Egyptians built their homes along the River Nile, near their crops.

The ancient Egyptians grew wheat to make bread.

Felucca boats sail on the River Nile.

7

The source of the Nile

Where a river begins is known as the river's **source**. At one time, it was thought that the River Nile started in the snow-capped Rwenzori Mountains in Uganda.

Rwenzori Mountains

This old map shows what people thought the Nile looked like.

For thousands of years, there have been **expeditions** to find the source of the Nile. Many failed because of injuries, illness, and even death. The landscape was difficult to travel through, too.

Early explorers

The Roman Emperor Nero sent soldiers to find the **source** of the Nile. They had to turn back because they could not travel through a **marshland** area called the **Sudd**. Plants grew so close together that the boats could not pass.

In 1770, Scotsman James Bruce found the source of the Blue Nile in Ethiopia.

"Sudd" means "barrier" in Arabic. The Sudd, in Sudan, was certainly a barrier to explorers!

Female traveller

In the early 1860s, Alexandrine-Pieternella-Françoise Tinné explored the White Nile in Sudan with her mother and aunt. At the time, women did not travel much and certainly not on their own!

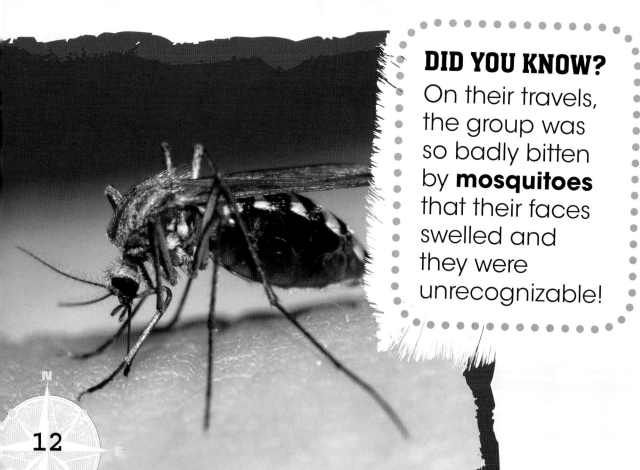

DID YOU KNOW?
On their travels, the group was so badly bitten by **mosquitoes** that their faces swelled and they were unrecognizable!

Alexandrine Tinné

Arguing over Lake Victoria

In 1857, John Hanning Speke and Richard Burton set out to find the **source** of the White Nile. Along the way, Burton became ill. Speke continued alone, and he reached Lake Victoria.

In 1858, Speke became the first European to see Lake Victoria, in Uganda.

Speke

Speke guessed that Lake Victoria was a source of the Nile. Burton did not believe him and the two men fell out.

A stone was laid to mark Speke's discovery of this source of the River Nile.

In 1862, John Hanning Speke discovered Ripon Falls on the coast of Lake Victoria. The water that flowed over these falls led to the White Nile. This was proof that Lake Victoria was the **source** of the Nile!

In 1860, Speke travelled to Africa again, this time with James Grant (on the left).

Another Nile source

British explorer Samuel White Baker explored the White Nile from 1861 to 1862. On his journey, he met some interesting people. The people Baker met used cows' urine and ash to colour their hair red!

Samuel White Baker

DID YOU KNOW?
Florence spoke many languages, rode camels and horses, and even carried a gun!

Samuel Baker's wife, Florence, travelled everywhere with him. It is thought she was once a **slave**, and that Baker met her while travelling in Europe.

In 1864, Baker found another lake and named it Lake Albert. Lake Albert gets water from the Victoria Nile, near to Murchison Falls.

This village is on the shores of Lake Albert.

Lost and found

David Livingstone set out to look for the Nile's **source** in 1866. He became extremely ill and lost touch with everyone he knew back in Britain. Many people thought he was dead.

An American man, Henry Stanley, was sent to find Livingstone. He found him in Tanzania. Livingstone was the only European there. Stanley asked a strange question: "Doctor Livingstone, I presume?". Livingstone died before reaching the Nile's source.

The real source?

In 2006, explorers found what they think is the furthest **source** of the River Nile, in Nyungwe Forest in Rwanda. During their journey, they wrecked a raft and a plane. One explorer broke his leg and the group was attacked by local rebels.

The source is known as the "Mac source". This is because all three men who discovered it have surnames beginning with "Mac"!

Around the Nile today

In 2006, oil was discovered under Lake Albert. A pipeline to move the oil needs to be built. It will have to go through swamps and mountains, and will cost lots of money.

The discovery of oil has caused arguments over where people can fish.

People drill for oil at Lake Albert.

Timeline

AD 66 Emperor Nero sends soldiers to find the **source** of the Nile.

1770 James Bruce announces he is the first European to reach the source of the Blue Nile.

1858 John Hanning Speke finds the source of the White Nile and calls it Lake Victoria.

1860s Alexandrine-Pieternella-Françoise Tinné explores the White Nile.

1861– 1864 The Bakers explore the Nile and discover Lake Albert.

1871 Henry Stanley "finds" Livingstone.

2006 The "Ascend the Nile" explorers find what they think is the furthest source of the Nile.

Explorer's checklist

If you want to go exploring, there are a few things you will need to take with you:

- map and compass
- food and water
- suncream
- phone
- hat
- cool clothing
- first-aid kit, including anti-**malaria** medicine
- **mosquito** net to keep away the mosquitoes.

Glossary

barrier something that blocks the way

crops plants that are grown for food, for example, wheat

expedition journey to explore a particular area

malaria serious disease that humans get after being bitten by a particular type of mosquito

marshland land that is often flooded with water and difficult to travel through

mosquito biting insect that sucks blood and spreads disease

slave person who is not paid for the work he or she does

source place from which a river begins. Rivers usually begin on high ground.

Sudd swampy area with thick plants near the River Nile

Find out more

Books

Children's Great Explorers Encyclopedia
(Parragon, 2010)

How to be an Explorer, Dugald Steer
(Templar, 2007)

The Nile (A River Journey), Rob Bowden
(Wayland, 2006)

Websites

www.bbc.co.uk/schools/riversandcoasts/ rivers/whatis_river/index.shtml
Learn about rivers on this BBC website.

www.woodlands-junior.kent.sch.uk/ Homework/egypt/nile.htm
Find out more about the River Nile on this website.

Index